BY MICHAEL GERBER

YO, SATURNALIA!

The War on Christmas...Santa Monica style

Now that the election is over, everybody here in Santa Monica is asking, "Do you think Stephen Miller's going to have to move back in with his parents?"

Actually, no. What we're all asking, over Zoom and Slack and even Peloton is, "What are *you* doing for the War on Christmas?"

There are as many ways to celebrate the War on Christmas as there are people who voted for Joe Biden. Here, on the sunkissed shores of Santa Monica Bay, where the Great White sharks are juveniles and almost never bite, two ways are considered traditional.

Going Back Home. Celebrating the holidays with the very people who drove you to California in the first place might seem like an odd way to celebrate. But this isn't a vacation, this is *magick*—and that extra "k" is for "kool." I have it on good authority (the guy at the tarot store) that enduring ice storms back in Shaker Heights is how we ensure another year of California sunshine. Similarly, being asked, "Aren't you *ever* going to have kids?" augurs a year of great personal creativity. And there's nothing better than a boozy lunch with a dead-eyed childhood friend to guarantee success in business. Or at least motivation to never, ever, *ever* give up on your dreams.

Christmas in Hawaii is the choice for people in showbiz, and you can make useful connections out by the pool. On the other hand, after a few umbrella drinks you may say the wrong thing to the wrong person and never work again. Welcome to Paranoia 'neath the Palms; wherever creatives gather, it's like high school had a baby with the Stasi.

For the rest of us, the War on Christmas is strictly a DIY affair. A lot of Santa Monicans celebrate Hanukkah, because they are Jewish or really like Tom Lehrer. Recently I've seen more people celebrating Kwanzaa. I don't know much about this holiday, but it seems to be Christmas as imagined by Earth Wind and Fire.

I forget the first year Kate and I decided to switch from Christmas to War on Christmas; I think it must've been after all our liberal radical Ph.D. friends held an impromptu re-education session in the breakroom of the old WeWork on the Third Street Promenade. For a few years, we celebrated one night's worth of Hanukkah, because our friend Barbara makes great latkes. But Hanukkah has

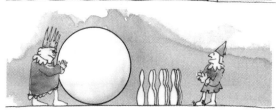

always felt like Shazam to Christmas' Superman, and I say: if you're going to War on Christmas, you gotta go Old School. So we picked Saturnalia.

For those of you who aren't ancient Romans, Saturnalia is a celebration of the god Saturn, spread over several December days full of feasting, gift-giving, gambling, and role-reversal. Masters would take orders from their slaves, which should give you an idea of just how drunk everyone got. Some lucky person would be picked "Lord of the Saturnalia," and everyone would have to obey them. Imagine 72 hours with that kind of power. Forced Jaegerbombs would be the least of it. "I command thee: *Put up this shelving!*"

Saturnalia worked fine for Kate and I until last year, when someone told our cats Max and Lola. The first night of Whiskas was okay (we put it on crackers), then the diarrhea went parabolic, which is when Kate and I realized just how small litter boxes really are. Lola declared herself "Lady of the Saturnalia" and made Kate play feather toy until she tore a rotator cuff. Max got addicted to online poker. We didn't even know he could *read*.

So this *annus horribilis* I'm declaring a whole new holiday: *Bystandermas*. Bystandermas is whatever you need it to be, for as long as you need it to be. The formal holiday begins on the anarchist Pyotr Kropotkin's birthday, December 9th, and ends five weeks later, on the birthday of LSD hero August Stanley Owsley (January 14th). During those five weeks, celebrants are obliged to do whatever makes them happy, whether that's paddleboarding with Great Whites or binge-watching *The Crown* or even sitting in a TGIFriday's back in Shaker Heights, listening to Mr. Dead Eyes explain how "the Asians" took his spot at Princeton.

During Bystandermas, everything is allowed. Give gifts! Demand gifts! Eat Whiskas on a Triscuit, if your guts can take it! If you're a subscriber SCOTUS will back you up, because "religious freedom"—right, Justice Alito? Justice Kavanaugh? Is Brett...asleep? Guess someone started Bystandermas a little early. So Merry Bystandermas everybody! May Kropotkin shower you with abundance, and Owsley keep you safely unbusted, until the next issue. **B**

"BOYLAN'S WRY WIT, WICKED SENSE OF HUMOR, AND UNIQUE WAY OF TURNING PHRASES SHINE THROUGH . . ."

~KIRKUS REVIEWS

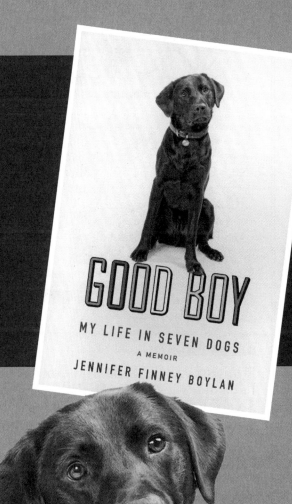

GOOD BOY

MY LIFE IN SEVEN DOGS

A NEW MEMOIR BY JENNIFER FINNEY BOYLAN, *NEW YORK TIMES* BESTSELLING AUTHOR OF *SHE'S NOT THERE: A LIFE IN TWO GENDERS*

"*Good Boy* is a warm, funny, instantly engaging testament to the power of love—canine and human—to ease us through life's radical transitions. And I say that as a cat person!"

~JENNIFER EGAN
Winner of the Pulitzer Prize and author of *A Visit from the Goon Squad* and *Manhattan Beach*

"Dogs help us understand ourselves: who we are, who we've been. They teach us what it means to love, and to be loved. They bear witness to our joys and sorrows; they lick the tears from our faces. And when our backs are turned, they steal a whole roasted chicken off the supper table."

~JENNIFER FINNEY BOYLAN

ON SALE
APRIL 21, 2020
PRE-ORDER NOW

CELADONBOOKS.COM/BOOKSHOP

TABLE OF CONTENTS

ROSS MACDONALD

The AMERICAN BYSTANDER

Founded 1981 by Brian McConnachie
#18 • Vol. 5, No. 2 • December 2020

EDITOR & PUBLISHER
Michael Gerber
HEAD WRITER Brian McConnachie
SENIOR EDITOR Alan Goldberg
ORACLE Steve Young
STAFF LIAR P.S. Mueller
INTREPID TRAVELER Mike Reiss
EAGLE EYES Patrick L. Kennedy
**AGENTS OF THE SECOND
BYSTANDER INTERNATIONAL**
Eve Alintuck, Melissa Balmain, Adrian
Bonenberger, Roz Chast, Rick Geary,
Sam Gross, Stephen Kroninger, Joey
Green, Matt Kowalick, Neil Mitchell,
Dalton Vaughn, and Maxwell Ziegler
MANAGING EDITOR EMERITA
Jennifer Finney Boylan
WARTIME CONSIGLIERA
Kate Powers
COVER BY
Rick Meyerowitz

ISSUE CONTRIBUTORS
Lucas Adams, Lou Beach, Barry Blitt,
George Booth, Tom Chitty, Marques
Duggans, Bob Eckstein, Emily Flake, E.R.
Flynn, James Finn Garner, Eric Gilliland,
Lance Hansen, Tim Harrod, Ron Hauge,
Sarah Hutto, Joe Janes, John Jonik, Ted
Jouflas, Sean Kelly, Peter Kuper, Ross
MacDonald, Merrill Markoe, Rick Mey-
erowitz, Ryan Nyburg, Oliver Ottitsch,
Lydia Oxenham, David Ostow, Jonathan
Plotkin, Lee Sachs, Don Steinberg, Mick
Stevens, D. Watson, and Andrew Weldon.

Lanky Bareikis, Jon Schwarz, Karen Back-
us, Ann McConnachie, Alleen Schultz,
Gray & Bernstein, Joe Lopez, Ivanhoe &
Gumenick, Greg & Trish G., Kelsey Hoke.
NAMEPLATES BY Mark Simonson
ISSUE CREATED BY Michael Gerber

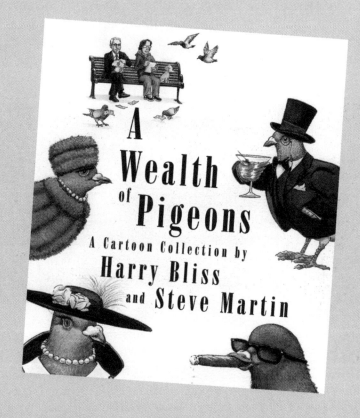

CARTOONS & ILLUSTRATIONS BY
Tom Chitty, D. Watson, Ross MacDonald, Barry Blitt, George Booth, Sam Gross, Lou Beach, Dalton Vaughn, Jonathan Plotkin, Lance Hansen, Peter Kuper, Rick Meyerwitz, Marques Duggans, Andrew Weldon, Emily Flake, Bob Eckstein, Ron Hauge, E.R. Flynn, Ted Jouflas.

Publisher's Note.

The last issue was mis-numbered, its spine reading "16" not "17." You may consider this our "inverted Jenny" and hoard copies accordingly. We have updated our processes to prevent this from reoccurring: first, the Editor's eyeballs have been replaced, and second, the number 17 is henceforth **strictly forbidden** from appearing in this magazine, in any form, for any reason, including matters of national security. *The American Bystander* expects **that** will show Mr. 17!

Sam's Spot

"Shouldn't you be delivering toys?"

COVER

With a ho, ho, ho and a pass the latkes Barbara, we proudly present "Santa, Cubed" by the legendary **RICK MEYEROWITZ**. Rick is one of my favorite Bystanders to work with; not only is his art pristine (which means I can relax and let him drive), every time we get on the phone, Rick makes me laugh. This is precious when you work from home, as everyone is discovering. I think this cover perfectly captures the utterly unique, multi-faceted holidays we're enduring this year, and thank Rick deeply for it. He doesn't know this, but I'm going to get him to do another one soon—I need an excuse to call!

ACKNO WLEDG MENTS

All material is ©2020 its creators, all rights reserved; please do not reproduce or distribute it without written consent of the creators and *The American Bystander*. The following material has previously appeared, and is reprinted here with permission of the author(s): Andrew Weldon's "Santa Pulls the Sleigh" first appeared in *The Age*. The first person to send me an email with the subject "I read the Acknowledgments" gets a free gift.

············◆············

THE AMERICAN BYSTANDER, *Vol. 5, No. 2*, (978-0-578-81556-5). Publishes ~5x/year. ©2020 by Good Cheer LLC. No part of this magazine can be reproduced, in whole or in part, by any means, without the written permission of the Publisher. For this and other queries, email *Publisher@ americanbystander.org*, or write: Michael Gerber, Publisher, *The American Bystander*, 1122 Sixth St., #403, Santa Monica, CA 90403. **Subscribe at www.patreon.com/bystander.** Other info can be found at www.americanbystander.org.

EARIOS

THE MARGARET CHO

ICONIC COMEDIAN MARGARET CHO TALKS WITH PEOPLE YOU KNOW, AND PEOPLE YOU SHOULD KNOW.

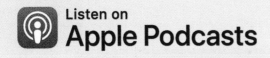 Listen on Apple Podcasts

 Spotify

acast

BY J. JONIK

HOLIDAY SPOTLIGHT

Some choose Xmas, others have Xmas thrust upon them

"It smells like a carrot."

"What are you gawking at!"

"Thank you, sir. And have a happy holiday of your choice!"

JOHN JONIK *has contributed cartoons for decades to many national publications, from A (Audubon) to Z (Z Magazine). He is based in Philadelphia.*

Gallimaufry

"It's time to preorder your Thanksgiving turkey!"
(sign spotted outside a butcher shop in September)

It's never too soon to preorder that turkey,
to pre-splurge on lights and white pine
for Christmas and New Year's
(not one year's, but two years'!),
to pre-pour the Valentine's wine.

So pre-April-Fool 'em! Pre-launch July rockets!
Pre-charbroil that Labor Day cow!
Don't waste precious minutes
on days that you're *in*: it's
too late to be having fun now.
—*Melissa Balmain*

A WALK ON CHRISTMAS EVE.

Walking through canyons of snow piled by shovel and plow I'm on my way to the drug store, the sky a twinkle and dark blue. It's early but it's winter so evening is here already and I like the dark, the streetlights making everything around me a stage set and the other actors are also bundled up and my part is to buy some aspirin. Down the street the library, the Hudson Branch, sits squat and homely as a basset hound, full of Freddy the Pig books and Penrod and Call of the Wild, books that drew me there often and pinned my attention, drew me more often than the large brick building catty-cornered—Benjamin Franklin Junior/Senior High School or opposite—Saint Stanislaus Roman Catholic Church or the quadrant's final anchor - Eddie's Corner, the lunch stop bunch stop for teens with rolled sleeves smoking at noon...I would join them in a few years, to savor the bitter cocktail of coffee and nicotine, the swagger and punch of pals.

But now I was just walking for my Mom, half on the sidewalk, half in my dreams, and what was I dreaming, the stars bright and heart embryonic and beating like a train yearning and hopeful and glad and mournful and stupid and wiser than the snow and the night. I wear gloves, no—mittens with reindeer running in wool and a woolen coat with big black buttons, gray with red trim at the collar and cuffs, a belt, and boots with buckles, and a watch cap, no ball on top, my hair peeking out and frozen, my nose and cheeks ablaze. Tracks in the snow like a railroad and I chug to the store and inside the long aisle split by shelving that holds shampoos and crèmes and notions and lotions and of course the candy and the medicine too.

I'm looking at the greens and bright blues, the hues and yellow letters and white labels and pink and the lady behind the counter asks after my mother and I tell her she's fine but leave out the part about the Xmas tree standing all crooked from my father's angry bump, drink in hand plaid shirt buttoned wrong, one button too many one button too few and my little sister crying and holding on to her Spanish skirt and hapless doll. Yeah, my mom is fine but has a headache you see and that's why I'm here and Merry Christmas to you and to Mr. The Pharmacist, too.

I march past the shoe repair where the old Italian man has had my black snap tongue shoes for too long now. I wear them with my black chinos, the ones with the buckle in the back and think I am Cool though in reality I'm a bit pudgy and my mother buys pants marked "Husky" at the Sears & Roebuck store. I wear glasses, too, though I often take them off, especially when I ride my bike to Patty's house, about a mile from mine. Her father doesn't like me,

"According to this, I'm 80% Jewish."

is it cuz I'm a slightly pudgy Polack who doesn't see well? She and I go next door to Jackie's house where Patty and I kiss and count each lip smack until we've reached one hundred, then take a breather and giggle, talk about the songs on the radio, Elvis Presley, Jackie doing homework and watching out for Patty's old man who won't look me in the eye even though I'm polite, maybe cuz he's not married anymore and divorce was still a weird thing back then and Patty is his only child and I am after all, chubby. Blocks from her house on the way back I retrieve my glasses and can see better now, can differentiate trees from lamp posts.

It's quiet at my house, the old man gone off to Sulkowski's or someplace and mom is sewing she's so good at it and my little sister is being little. I'll work on my model of the USS Forrestal, the world's largest aircraft carrier which I'll put next to my already assembled bristle of rockets, Monogram's Missile Arsenal, my favorite being the Winged Snark but pretty good too is Thor and Jupiter, the big daddys. There's thirty-one of them in all, on a clear plastic stand that my sister will smash later in the year, then hit me in the head with a telephone receiver for good measure. It's tough sharing a room with a woman.

But… I am her companion and break-fast maker and walk-to-school protector and I throw a guy down in the snow who hit her with a snowball, I chase him and knock him over push him and hold him so she can smash snow into his face and I'm her hero brother you see. I'm also a hero crossing guard at school with a white belt that has a special way of being folded and it hangs from my cool pants with a clip but I am relieved of this duty after a few weeks for fighting.

I get home from the drug store and there is old man Novak slipping on the icy sidewalk, drunk again along the side of our house, that narrow walk, on the way to his third of our three family building, he falls and passes out and I kick him in the ribs then go tell his Mrs. Novak where he is and she gives me ten cents, a dime, and wishes me a Merry Christmas, nice lady. He was a mean prick and I was glad when they moved away but she was ok.

I'm inside our warm house now and run water for a bath in the bathroom where sharp little points stick out of the pink sandpaper-like plaster of the walls and I scratch my back against them, naked, and from three feet away try to pee into the bathtub and mother says from the other room, the other room with the wall paper, what are you doing

in there and I say I'm getting clean for Christmas Eve, Ma, getting clean for Christmas.

—*Lou Beach*

TWO CORINTHIANS.

Two Corinthians walk into a taverna. The first Corinthian says, "Say, buddy, what's the difference between a Cynic and a Stoic? The second Corinthian says, 'That's an easy one, pal. A Stoic is what brings the little babies and a Cynic is what you wash the little babies in."

Two Corinthians walk into a taverna. They're both heretics. One guy's a Manichean and the other guy is a Gnostic. The serving wench gives the Manichean a retsina, but points to a sign over the bar that says, GNOSTIC, GNO SERVICE.

Two Corinthians walk into a bar. They do this daily until some kindly pagan raises the bar.

Two Corinthians, Paul and Simon, walk into a taverna. Paul says, "Say, you're new around here, ain't you? Where do you hail from you from?" Simon says, "Athens." Paul says, "What line of work are you in?" Simon says, "I'm a metaphysician." Paul says, "Let me buy you a retsina! I've never meta-physician I didn't like."

—*Sean Kelly*

UNPRODUCED SPECIALS.

Your Skin is a Prison, Charlie Brown
Guns Have No Morals, Charlie Brown
Ghosts are Just Memories, Charlie Brown
If You Listen to a Grave You Can Hear It Scream, Charlie Brown
God Hates a Coward, Charlie Brown
Death is No Escape, Charlie Brown
If Hell Wants Him it Can Have Him, Charlie Brown
The Blood Does Not Wash Away Easily, Charlie Brown
To Be a King is to Be a Murderer, Charlie Brown
You Only Adversary is Time, Charlie Brown
Life is a Disease, Charlie Brown
The Temperature at Which Bones Burn, Charlie Brown

"*We have somehow angered the nation's bowlers.*"

SANTA'S LEAST FAVORITE ELVES

EUGENE
Labor
Organizer

TRACEY
Eggnog
addict

CLAYTON
Embezzler

PEPPERMINT
Dating Santa's
daughter

Hell is In Your Own Skull, Charlie Brown

When Angels Die They Die Screaming, Charlie Brown

The World Died a Generation Ago, Charlie Brown

Let Poison Be Your Succor, Charlie Brown

The Bell Tolls for All Humanity, Charlie Brown

Burn Down Your Own Brain, Charlie Brown

—*Ryan Nyburg*

EVERYTHING IS GOING TO BE OKAY™

As Chief Spokesindividual for the United States Center for Disease Control (acting), it goes without saying that we applaud the tens of U.S. citizens who are continuing to wear masks over their noses and mouths to prevent the spread of COVID-19. Thank you. Now, there have been rumblings—In These Challenging Times™—that the CDC has been "hamstrung" or maybe "gutted" or even "emasculated" and "bitchslapped" by the current administration. But I'm here to tell you nothing could be further from the truth. We are simply Broadening the Parameters® by which we "control"…y'know: disease. At our center. For disease control.

Anyway. In that spirit, let me also take a moment to praise and honor a different and even larger number of brave Americans who are doing their part in keeping our country as safe as possible during these end days. These heroes listened to medical professionals and informed governmental leaders and—fashion be damned—are heading out of the house proudly and without complaint wearing their neck masks.

Fact: Adam's apples sweat. Buckets. Those neck masks protect me from their nape droplets splashing across the sidewalk and landing on my stupidly unmasked forehead, infecting my hairline with disease. Is the word "splashing" too much of an exaggeration? Not when the considerate neck mask wearer is jogging. And quite often he is.

Other benefits of wearing a neck mask? Wattle hiding. Let's face it, we've all put on a few pounds during the pandemic. And most of it went to our necks. "Did you get the Covid-19?" every clever person says, referring to gaining 19 pounds during the pandemic. Every single clever person says that. They say that and then point to their stomach. Every time. (It's amazing how—even during a global tragedy—American wits are not backing down.) But now these honorable gentlepeople can hide that extra neck fat with their neck mask! Classic win-win. For medicine *and* body image. I don't want to be lying in a refrigerated truck with my wrinkly neck exposed for all to see. When a loved one comes to identify me, I want them to look away in horror because I'm dead, not because my neck is disgusting.

I further commend the caring citizens who, instead of the neck mask, really go the whole nine yards to serve their communities and wear a wrist mask. It's good to have alternatives in a pandemic and they have found it. *Fact:* Tops of hands sweat. Buckets. Especially when jogging. And they usually are. So, I walk down the street feeling protected and safe as these fit patriots rush up from behind, without warning, proudly wearing that wrist mask. At first, I'm absolutely startled and might even spit out a swear word because wow, why would someone do that? Especially now. Just, without warning, dash by me, huffing and puffing, grunting out from their mouths and noses, "splashing" (see above), without so much as an "Excuse me." I mean, what the hell? How were you raised, jogger? Again, just…wow. But then I see their wrist mask fully in place, and my shoulders go down and I sigh with relief. They are paying attention. My mistake! I'm sorry I was in your way and you had no other choice than to bump into me. And pass off some sweat. You're looking good, buster! Keep pushing yourself! And me out of the way! See you at the marathon, negative testing permitting! Or not!

It goes without saying that I also praise the heck out of the one-ear-dangling jowl mask wearers. Fact: Jowls etc.

And, hey, I get it. If you have to smoke, you have to smoke.

Note that the CDC approves of all these wide-ranging changes. At least that's what we've been told to do. So, if we can keep our diligence throughout this incredibly dangerous time with people dying and no end in sight, since mid-March, while things get worse and worse and worse almost everywhere throughout the entire world and Georgia…keep wearing your masks! Y'know, at least somewhere on your body. The CDC officially says "It doesn't matter where anymore." It's the headline on our website. I mean…I think we still have a website. And we'll lick this yet! (And yet, the problem with wearing a face mask is that licking is impossible, but since so few opt for that type of mask, we just might be in this

for quite some time.)

I will be happy to answer any questions via the Formerly Functioning USPS©.

—*Eric Gilliland*

I DON'T WANT YOUR FAMILY CHRISTMAS PHOTOS.

Last December, the OxenMan and I sent handwritten Christmas cards to our loved ones. In an age of impersonal mass-printed cards with generic, non-denominational messaging, we wanted to add a personal touch.

We prepped our list of the lucky few who would receive a card, and I took great delight in eliminating names from that list. Who truly *deserved* our priceless Christmas messages?

Once the list was complete (about 50 names in all), the real work began. We spent hours composing specific, personal messages. Each message was original, tailored to the recipient, and tried to strike a nice balance—sincere but amusing; full of relationship context, but also touching on contemporary events. We didn't type out what to say beforehand. The messages, we thought, should overflow from our hearts. As a result, we couldn't write more than two cards a night—the emotional exertion was too much.

And what, for our troubles, did we get in return? Glossy family photos with boughs of holly in the corners, courtesy of Costco. Or Shutterstock. Or another capitalist Grinch masquerading as Santa's helper.

These photo cards came in a few pre-dictable varieties:

- *family in matching Christmas pajamas*
- *new baby, sometimes in Christmas pajamas*
- *collages of Facebook profile pictures (no attempt at Christmas anything)*

What were they all lacking? A personal touch. There were no notes. Sometimes, very occasionally, the sender would undistract themselves long enough to scrawl "Love, the _____ family."

I did not feel any love. In fact, I was hurt. Here I'd spent all this time trying to share something *real*, and I'd gotten an automated response.

For example, I'd written that Lisa was "a lifelong friend," and that "I was grateful she welcomed me into her family when I first moved to town." What I got back was a picture of her family in Harry Potter pajamas. She didn't even hand-address the envelope.

Then there was the college friend I'd reconnected with. Earlier that year, we vowed to exchange Christmas cards, and I hoped this would be the re-kindling of kindred spirits. I told her I "admired her beautiful family," and that "the stories about her son struck a chord in my heart." She wrote back, "Happy Holidays!"

I considered giving her a pass because

she has three young children, but then I thought: shouldn't she be setting a better example for them? If, twenty years from now, those kids text her an AI-generated string of emojis on December 24, 11:59 p.m., well, she only has herself to blame!

In an age of easily accessible digital photos, shouldn't the point of holiday cards be to share honest, individual thoughts with those we claim to care about? Christmas should be a time to push ourselves to dig deep, to give more.

That said, I need a break. The OxenMan and I will not be sending cards this Christmas. Writing individual thoughtful messages is exhausting. And time consuming. I don't have the emotional stamina. My hand's cramping just thinking about it.

Please consider this your 2020 Christmas card. You can imagine us in matching Harry Potter pajamas.

—*Lydia Oxenham*

WERNER HERZOG ON LEAVES.

A leaf falls to the ground.

These photosynthesizing mechanisms, now remnants, barely move but for a passing wind.

This annual ritual indicates the cyclical hibernation, preparing for the dark, cold winter.

Alas, in modern society, the leaf cannot be left to lie in its natural state.

Manual raking, a technique which dates back thousands of years, is now pointless.

Today, machinery, creating a wind of over 150 miles per hour, uses tremendous force to scatter handfuls of leaves a few feet at a time.

This grating two-cycle engine, destroys the autumn silence with its persistent drone.

Leaves fly haphazardly like soldiers strewn from a nuclear blast.

Finally, like a mountain of rubble from an explosion, a pile of leaves remain.

Are the leaves and the leaf blowers any wiser?

—*Lee Sachs*

Sacred Snowman burial Grounds

THE MUST-READ BOOKS OF 2021.

My new year's resolution is to read every book that will end up on next year's "Best of" lists. This resolution has nothing to do with becoming a more well-read person, and everything to do with my fear of inadequacy.

Since the lists don't exist yet, I'll have to read every book, just in case. It'll take hours of eye strain. I may go blind. I'll have no time for the OxenMan. Books are my husband now. And by consuming only what's popular, I'll lose any shred of individuality. But it'll be worth it when I can say I've read everything an unpaid intern at Buzzfeed deemed important.

I want my 2021 boiled down to a series of media-approved literary experiences. Will you join me?

—*Lydia Oxenham*

LAST WORDS.

Wilde and the wallpaper got into a tussle
Fields took a shot at a city.
Walt wrote, quite cryptically, two words:
"Kurt Russell."
And Papa bid farewell to Kitty.

—*Lance Hansen*

NEW YORK IS STILL ALIVE, MUCH LIKE THESE FORTY-YEAR-OLD SEA MONKEYS.

When I first moved to New York, it was during the Carter Administration, and he'd just murdered that rabbit in his dinghy. You're probably too young to remember that, but I remember, because my uncle was married to that rabbit's cousin and, well, his wife was never the same. Didn't speak a word the rest of her natural life, which was only about year, on account of her being a rabbit. Don't look at me like that! It was the '70s. Yes, okay? We ate rabbit. We had to. We didn't have the fancy mock meats you kids have today, so we ate rabbit. And sometimes, just sometimes, if you were lucky, you met a very special rabbit, and you tied the knot. Life is short. We couldn't afford to be picky about supper or wives.

"It's just that we've been planning our thing for a really long time."

After my uncle's wife died—or, "Aunt Rabbit," as we called her—I invited him to visit me on the island of Manhattan, where I'd taken up residence in the bathroom of a Chinese restaurant on Canal Street. The family who ran the restaurant never noticed me, I was that good of a tenant. To repay them for being my unwitting landlords, I whispered positive subliminal messages in their ears every night, which in turn, boosted their self esteem. I don't know if their self esteem actually needed boosting—they seemed pretty comfortable in their life stations—but I just figured it was my way of leaving a good mark. New York was like that back then—we actually *cared*.

Eventually I moved out of the Chinese restaurant bathroom and into a car parked under an overpass in a very trendy part of Brooklyn called, CAPAWBO, or Car Parked Under Williamsburg Bridge Overpass. I'll never forget that day. I thought, "This is the greatest city in the world!" I even splurged and went out and got myself some sea monkeys to put on the dashboard. See? Some forty-odd years later and they're still kicking. You just need to give the jar a good shake and they

still dance around.

But now we've got people saying New York is dead, all because of a little virus. You cannot be serious! Look, I know this is a tough time. Most of the cars have been towed from under the bridge overpasses, no one lets you take your catnaps in the Chinese restaurant bathrooms, and all the sea monkeys are being bought up by the hospitals.

And then there's this virus. Well, this isn't the first time New York has seen a virus. Let me remind you of a little sickness called Scurvy.

When the first settlers arrived in New York, they were exhausted and their gums were bleeding because they'd forgot to pack oranges for their trip. The New York harbor was teeming with Scurvy! I mean, sure it wasn't a *true* virus, on account of being a vitamin deficiency, but still, it made everyone really self-conscious about their gums. Dating was a nightmare during that time, for many reasons including the bathing issue, but especially the Scurvy. But the point is, we got through it. New York Strong—isn't that what they say?

Hell, I have Scurvy right now. But you don't see me complaining about my gums bleeding and heading off to

Florida to take advantage of their orange surplus. *Hell no!* I'm a New Yorker! We live in bathrooms and our gums bleed! Why, just today while I was putting out a fire in my living room because someone threw a lit cigarette out of a Saab as they drove over the bridge, I thought to myself, "Yep! New York's still got it, Baby!" I could not put the fire out and the car unfortunately exploded, but I'm not worried! I'm a New Yorker, dammit! A New Yorker with unusually advanced Scurvy that is probably eligible for some type of city-funded housing.

So if you'll excuse me, I'm going to go look into that right now. And you enjoy your cushy life in some place that will never have half the spunk, bridge overpasses, or Chinese restaurant bathrooms as New York. But do me a favor, will you? Take this jar of sea monkeys with you. The housing I'm applying for doesn't allow pets and these guys deserve an easier life. Oh would you look at that. The jar must have cracked during the car explosion. Come to think of it—this would make a really good sourdough starter.

Never mind.

—*Sarah Hutto*

DUM SPIRO SPERO.

When we get the vaccine
Then *adieu* quarantine
Take me off this machine
For it's all been foreseen
When we get the vaccine.

When we get the vaccine
We'll abstain from caffeine
Keep a healthy routine
Eat organic cuisine
How we'll saunter and preen
How we'll strut and careen
And we'll splice every gene
When we get the vaccine.

The New Deal will be green
And the air will be clean
They will lift every lien
We'll be terribly keen
And yet calm and serene
There'll be nothing obscene
Not a word or a scene
On the stage or the screen
To be sinfully seen
When we get the vaccine.

So come on Eileen
Fetch your old tambourine
And we'll all reconvene
At the stage door canteen
Every adult and teen
Will begin the beguine
They won't need Vaseline
If you know what I mean
When we get the vaccine

—*Sean Kelly* B

Follow Peter Kuper,

REUBEN AND EISNER AWARD-WINNING AUTHOR,

into the heart of an immense darkness

**In stores
11.5.2019**

"Not only a triumph of graphic art but a compelling
work of literary interpretation. [Kuper] has designed a
masterful synthesis that retains Conrad's language while
pressing beyond the limits of Conrad's vision."

—MAYA JASANOFF, COOLIDGE PROFESSOR OF HISTORY,
HARVARD UNIVERSITY, FROM THE FOREWORD

"As a deeply uncomfortable depressed Midwest person, I relate to this excruciatingly hilarious book more than I'd like to admit."

—SAMANTHA IRBY, *New York Times* best-selling author

"Hilarious, warm, relatable, confessional, and emotional. Her writing leaps off the page! But not literally. That would be horrible. Imagine writing leaping off the page, soiling your house. Just awful."

— MEGAN AMRAM, writer/producer of *The Good Place* & *The Simpsons*

ESSAYS on the AWKWARD, UNCOMFORTABLE, SURPRISINGLY REGULAR PARTS of BEING HUMAN

~ including ~

My Dog Explains My Weekly Schedule • Depression Isn't a Competition, but, Like, Why Aren't I Winning? • Mustache Lady • White Friend Confessional • Treating Objects Like Women

HarperOne   *An Imprint of HarperCollinsPublishers*   www.harperone.com

BY STEVE YOUNG

RENTAL SANTA SUIT INVENTORY NOTES

Attention all A-1 Costume Rental staff! As we head into the holiday season, please refer to the following inventory notes when renting the Santa suits!

Suit 1: This is one of the more popular suits and is to be offered to the average customer if available. Shows only minor wear and is of nice quality.

Suit 2: Very similar to Suit 1, except for the extremely strong odor of onions which cleaning has been unable to remove. Generally only appropriate for rental to Mr. Van Vonk, who no longer has a sense of smell after the boating accident.

Suit 3: This Santa suit, consisting solely of the white wig and beard, is the suit we offer to nudists.

Suit 4: Standard suit, in fair condition with minor rips and holes. Rentable, though some consider it "cursed" because Mr. Van Vonk was wearing it at the time of the boating accident.

Suit 5: This like-new suit only fits elk, moose, and other large ungulates. NOT FOR GIRAFFE USE WITHOUT LEG AND NECK EXTENSIONS, AVAILABLE AT EXTRA CHARGE

Suit 6: A stylish, high-quality Santa suit which is often requested by fans of the adult film it appears in, *Oh God Oh God Ye Merry Gentlemen*. REQUIRES EXTRA DEEP-CLEANING UPON RETURN

Suit 7: A special suit made of red neoprene, designed for scuba diving. The fur trim requires thorough drying before storage to avoid mildew. Also, as we learned from the 2017 incident, the pockets must be checked for fish.

Suit 8: Clearly identifiable by the large, prominent "SUIT 8" emblems on the chest, back, arms, legs, and hat. Excellent condition; very rarely rented.

Suit 9: Standard Santa suit appearance, but with built-in athletic cup for protection during hockey, cricket, and fencing events.

Suit 10: Similar to Suit 9, but with larger size cup, and the hat has a longer droopy part.

Suit 11: Standard Santa suit, good quality, but DO NOT RENT AS IT HAS BEEN PERMANENTLY RESERVED BY MR. VAN VONK TO BE BURIED IN

Suit 12: Custom-tailored suit of red-dyed genuine reindeer hide. For darker scenarios in which a Santa wishes to warn of "what happens to those who cross me."

Suit 13: Traditional suit, but proportioned for a renter with an extremely muscular athletic build, having only one arm (left) and an enormous head, of significantly below average height, and willing to accept some mustard stains.

Suit 14: Medium size Santa suit constructed of heavy-duty flame- and heat-resistant material, designed for wear while fighting oil well fires. NOTE: Warn renter that beard will ignite.

Suit 15: Good-quality average size suit UNAVAILABLE UNTIL FURTHER NOTICE AS IT IS EVIDENCE IN A FEDERAL EXTORTION/ROBBERY/MURDER CASE

Suit 16: "Conceptual" Santa suit consisting of dozens of white beards, and a beard made of red fabric. Seldom requested.

Consult management if you have any questions. Let's just get through Christmas, and then we'll worry about the nightmare of Baby New Year. **B**

STEVE YOUNG *(@pantssteve) is a veteran* **Letterman** *writer who's also written for* **The Simpsons**. *He's the main subject of the award-winning documentary,* **Bathtubs Over Broadway**.

BY LOU BEACH

THANK YOU, MR. BELUSHI

In Hollywood, it's not who you know, but who they think you are

There is a venerated restaurant in Hollywood, right on the Boulevard, that's been there for close to one hundred years, serving chops and flannel cakes and the best martini in town.

If you enter through the back, from the parking lot, you descend a short flight of stairs and move past the kitchen, the restroom doors, the phone booth and the little wall rack that holds picture postcards of the place, and enter a long, softly lit room with red leather banquettes and dark wood paneling. A counter flanks a wall, a good place for late breakfast.

There is another, larger room as well. It's where the bar resides and behind it, the red-jacketed barkeep. Moving through both rooms are bow-tied waiters, many who've worked there for decades. They recognize you and remember your name and food and beverage preferences. Between the two rooms is a counter with a cash register and the reservation book and the gentlemen who for many years would greet you at the front.

The amiable fellow's name was Phillip and he was the *maître d'*. Of medium height, slightly portly, Phillip would guide you effortlessly to the booth where the others in your party awaited, or apologize that the table wasn't ready and lead you to the bar.

He was an old school gentleman, impeccably groomed, with a kindly twinkle behind his thin-rimmed glasses. His suits were dark blue or gray, set off by a well-knotted tie.

I frequented the place in those days, often with a close friend, well known in the joint, who worked in the biz. I happened to pay for our meal one time with a credit card and I believe this is what started the whole business. I think Phillip glanced at my name on the small receipt and mistook it for that of Jim Belushi, to whom I bore a very slight resemblance. Our names share a few letters, and a like-sounding syllable. After that, Phillip began addressing me as "Mr. Belushi".

Thinking it quite funny, neither my friends nor I did anything to dispel his misapprehension.

"You are looking well, Mr. Belushi."

"No one in the place looks as good as you, Phillip," I said.

"You are too kind, Mr. Belushi. How is the new show coming along?" he'd say, handing me the large menu.

"Fine, just fine, Phillip, thank you."

And so it went for about a year. Even if I didn't have a reservation and showed up with a group, Phillip would see to it that we were seated promptly. Waiting patrons would grumble, perhaps wondering who I might be, but he paid them no heed.

Just before Christmas that year, the joke started getting thin for me and I wondered how to come clean to Philip without hurting his feelings or humiliating him. While walking through a department store looking for a gift for my wife, I came upon the men's tie counter. Aha, I thought, I'll give Phillip a couple of ties and sign my name to the gift card in large, legible letters.

We'd both be saved embarrassment and I could go back to being just plain old non-Belushi me.

I chose two ties, expensive ones that I thought complemented Phillip's suits and had them gift-wrapped. I took the package home and wrote a note in my best fourth grade script: "Phillip, please accept this small token in appreciation of your kindness and generosity. Very best wishes for a merry Christmas," and signed my name. Large.

I asked my wife if my name was legible.

"You could read it from across the street," she said.

I met my pal at the restaurant and as we were sliding into the booth, Phillip walked over to say hello. I presented him with the gift.

"Merry Christmas, Philip."

"Thank you, thank you Mr. Belushi, so much," he said and tucked the box under his arm.

"I will put it beneath the tree when I get home tonight." He hurried away to greet a large party at the door.

I didn't return until the end of January. As I approached the booth where my friend was waiting, Phillip rushed up to me.

"I love the ties," he said, shaking my hand. "Thank you, Mr. Belushi!"

B

LOU BEACH *is an artist, writer, and award-winning illustrator living in Los Angeles.*

BY JOE JANES

CLARENCE'S REPORT

*You think **that's** a wonderful life? Wait'll you get a load of Juniper P. Moneylumps*

Joseph! Joseph! It's me, Clarence! I hate to bother you, but I wanted to ask about those wings…

[CLARENCE listens intently to ST. JOSEPH, whom we do not hear.]

Did things work out with George Bailey?…Well, sort of…

[Pause]

What do I mean? He's very happy now, and doesn't want to jump off the bridge and kill himself anymore. So mission accomplished, I'd say! My wing size is six-and-a-half, narrow. But of course you knew that already.

[CLARENCE listens intently to ST. JOSEPH, whom we do not hear.]

Well… No. I didn't change things back exactly. I left him at Nick's Bar. It was the strangest thing, Joseph: once George realized no one knew who he was, he started to really *enjoy* it. George Bailey, our George Bailey, began walking around the bar telling everyone, "My name is Pierre Alejandro Magellan. I'm an adventurer who has travelled all around the world. I've seen sights, eaten foods, and made love to women like you wouldn't believe." People are buying him drinks in exchange for his stories. He's making friends like mad. Happy ending, wouldn't you say?

[Pause]

I thought the same thing, so I pulled him aside on the way to the john. George *did* say he missed his family, but is excited to not have that responsibility anymore.

[Pause]

No, that *isn't* how he said it. He said, quote, "I'm so goshdarn glad to be rid of that albatross of a wife, and and and those runny-nosed naked mole rats running all over the house! And speaking of, that firetrap is a rickety old money pit that smells worse than Uncle Billy's longjohns!"

[Pause]

No, he wasn't finished. He also told Ernie and Bert they were "just a couple of fancy boys and that they should just get to smooching already!" That came out of nowhere. I think he had been holding on to that for a while. However, Ernie and Bert did seem happy, making out in the back of Ernie's cab.

[Pause]

Oh, I don't agree, Joseph. I'm *glad* George ended up at Nick's. It could be so much worse; right before that, we were in a dance hall. "A dime a dance is a really good value," he said, "and it keeps people employed. Especially the floozies! Right, floozy?" He claimed it was his civic duty—and the floozy agreed. We got out just before the cops busted the joint.

[Pause]

No, George still *hates* Potter. I thought we'd really done something, showing him how important he was to Bedford Falls, which is now Pottersville. But then he gave Potter a stock tip on Sam Wainwright's business that will make a fortune. In gratitude, Potter's wired over enough money for a trip around the world for George. Or "Juniper"—he introduced himself to Mr. Potter as "Juniper P. Moneylumps." He has several different aliases, now.

[Pause]

Yes, well, he also called the SEC. Potter'll be nabbed for insider trading by Monday. "By which time, Clarence, I will be in Suriname."

[Pause]

Yes, I reminded George that without him, his brother died and the druggist, Mr. Gower, poisoned a lot of people and ended up being the town drunk. And that Zuzu's petals don't exist because she doesn't exist. He got a very somber look on his face and was quiet for a long time. And then he said, "So, I'm free?" I said, "I guess so, George." And then he smiled and said, "Call me Demetrick, comrade."

[Pause]

I made one last-ditch effort to get through to him. I gave him my copy of *The Adventures of Tom Sawyer*. He said he had read it. I said, "So it made you realize the value of relationships and connection?" and Demetrick or Juniper or Magellan just said, "Nah, I liked the running away part." When I got my book back, he'd circled all the dirty words.

[Pause]

That's one way of looking at it. But he clearly thinks this new life is wonderful. So, Joseph: do I get my wings, or do I have to call my lawyer? **B**

JOE JANES *(@joejanes1065) is an adjunct professor in the comedy program at Columbia College Chicago and teaches at The Second City Training Center in Chicago. You can lightly stalk him on the socials.*

BY MIKE REISS

SANTA'S BROTHER SANDY

Surf's up, hodads—he's here to save Christmas

Whenever it's Christmas, wherever there's snow
And chimneys and children, Santa will go.

But when he reached Bali, a very warm land,
His sleigh and his reindeer got stuck in the sand.

It soon would be dawn and he still had to reach
The millions of children who lived near a beach.

Santa sweated and fretted—'twas ninety degrees!
And his reindeer had sunk in the sand to their knees!

He pulled out his phone as he choked back his tears
And he called up a man he had not seen in years:

"You've got to save Christmas! You must hear my plea!"
In moments, a giant clam rose from the sea…

The clam opened up and a man was inside
"Ho ho ho," Santa cried. "Hey hey hey," he replied.

He looked like Saint Nick, but with muscles and abs
And shorts decorated with mussels and crabs.

He was called Sandy Claus—he was Santa's kid brother!
And like many brothers, they fought with each other:

"Sandy, you're lazy! You should get a job!"
"Santa, you're crazy! You blubbery slob!

Santa, you see, was a hard-working man
While the only thing Sandy worked on was his tan.

But Santa told Sandy, "I'm not here to fight.
The whole world is counting on your help tonight.
You've spent your life on the sand and the sea.
You know these islands much better than me.
I'm asking your help to deliver these toys
To the fun-loving girls and the sun-loving boys."

Sandy said, "Dude." That was it. Nothing more.
Then he picked up the toy-bag and walked to the shore

He hopped on his surfboard and paddled away
While a team of sea creatures pulled him like a sleigh:

"On Sunfish! On Sailfish! On Seahorse and Seal!
On Porpoise! And Tortoise! On Tuna and Eel!"

He brought toys to Haiti, Hawaii, Aruba
Tahiti and Tonga, Bermuda and Cuba.

He visited houses and huts and cabanas
Where kids left him coconut milk and bananas.
And Spam. These kids really love Spam.

He surfed through typhoons and monsoons and a drought,
Surfed in a whale's mouth and then surfed out its spout.

He had one island left—it was called Zanzibar.
But a fog had rolled in that was thicker than tar.

Sandy said, "Electric eel
Won't you do your glowing deal?"

It sizzled and fizzled and glowed like the sun
And thanks to that eel, Sandy got the job done.

He got back to Bali at six in the morning.
And he and his brother watched Christmas Day dawning.

Sandy said, "Santa, I've been a real jerk.
I just never knew you could have fun at work!

"So maybe you'll let me help out every year
While you sit on the beach and chill out with your deer.

"I'm sorry I called you a slob. That was rude."
And Santa replied with a single word:
        "Dude."   B

MIKE REISS *has won four Emmys and a Peabody during his twenty-six years writing for* The Simpsons. *Reiss also co-created* The Critic, *and created Showtime's hit cartoon* Queer Duck *(about a gay duck).*

BY DON STEINBERG

APOCRYPHAL TALES REVISITED

Stories of the Season

SILENT CAL

President Calvin Coolidge was widely known as a man of few words. At a Christmas party for Washington VIPs, a young couple saw him and devised a wager.

The couple approached Coolidge. "Mr. President," the woman said, "I just bet my husband $50 that I could get you to say three words."

Coolidge looked at her and said, "You lose."

The woman laughed. "How disappointing!" she said, extending her hand. "My name is Eleanor Roosevelt, and this is Franklin. Could you tell me where to find the ladies' room?"

Coolidge opened his mouth, then realized the woman's gambit. Slowly, silently, he raised his middle finger.

Franklin laughed.

YOUNG GEORGE WASHINGTON

When he was only six years old, George Washington received a hatchet as a Christmas present. He put it to use by enthusiastically chopping down his father's prized cherry tree.

SANTA COOLIDGE: *"Ho ho."*

Washington's dad was furious. "Who did this?"

"I cannot tell a lie. I did it with my little hatchet," George confessed.

"You *what?*" the elder Washington said. "Chopping down a tree single-handedly is difficult even for a grown man. We should enter you in some kind of competition."

THE PICASSO NAPKIN

In Paris in December 1934, an older gentleman and his companion were having lunch at a restaurant when a young man approached.

"I'm sorry to bother you," the young man said, "but are you Pablo Picasso?"

The older man smiled thinly, accustomed to the interruption. "Yes."

"Oh my," the young man said. "I'd never bother you, but my wife is your biggest fan. She's very ill and doesn't have much longer to live. It would mean so much to her if you could draw her a picture, even on a napkin."

Picasso sighed and put down his utensils. He fished in his jacket for a pencil and spread his napkin on the table. He quickly drew a series of shapes that resembled a woman's face, signed his name, and pushed the napkin toward the young man. "That'll be $1,000," Picasso said.

"$1,000? It only took you two minutes to draw!"

"Yes," Picasso answered, "but it took me forty years to be able to draw it in two minutes."

The young man sighed. "Forty years, what a gift. My poor wife is not likely to make it even to Christmas. It would cheer her so much to get a free drawing from Pablo Picasso."

Picasso laid his hand over the napkin drawing. "I'm sorry to hear that you are being so frugal about your wife's dying wish."

"How about three hundred?"

Picasso agreed and handed over the illustration for $300.

The young man rejoined his own dining companion. He grinned across the table and spoke in a low voice. "I just got a signed Picasso for three hundred bucks!" he whispered.

Back at the other table, the old man's lunch date gave him a quizzical look. "Why did you do that?" she asked him.

"Everybody thinks I look like Picasso," he said. "Why not make something off of it?"

THE CHURCHILL INSULT

British Prime Minister Winston Churchill was famous for his withering insults. At a Christmas party he was behaving boorishly when a woman approached him.

"Winston, you are drunk, disgustingly drunk!" she proclaimed.

Churchill slowly removed the cigar from his mouth and scowled.

"My dear madam, you are ugly," he said in his stentorian voice. "In the morning, I shall be sober, and you will still be ugly."

The woman smiled.

"Thank you," she said. "I bet Coolidge over there $50 that you would insult me."

Churchill laughed. Franklin laughed. And Eleanor, smiling at Coolidge, silently raised her middle finger. **B**

DON STEINBERG *(@WriteDon) has written for* **The New Yorker**, **GQ**, *and* **The Wall Street Journal**. *He publishes the humor magazine* **Meanwhile**.

THE DAIRY RESTAURANT

BEN KATCHOR

Through text and drawings, award-winning author Ben Katchor retells the history of where we choose to eat and illuminates the historical confluence of events and ideas that led to the proliferation of dairy restaurants in America.

A UNIQUE HISTORY of a beloved culinary institution

Schocken
>nextbook

Dairy Restaurant, 4901 16th Avenue, Brooklyn, Borough Park. Opened in 1968 by Tillie and Jacob Lieberman. Currently operated by their son Shloime Lieberman and his wife Roz. A popular corner breakfast and lunch place with tables for twelve and a counter for ten features omelets, soups, and sandwiches. Angelo Saavedra, who came from Mexico, started as their egg chef in 2000 and uses individual frying pans, not a grill. Like most dairy restaurants, they never felt the need for official certification, and to this day, there hangs in their window a statement of their own devising that attests to their compliance with dietary laws.

The B&H Dairy Lunch, 127 Second Avenue, New York, opened 1937 or 1938. A remnant of the Second Avenue Yiddish rialto, the B&H catered to a new generation of young Lower East Siders who appreciated its inexpensive vegetarian fare. The sign outside reads "dairy lunch"; a neon sign in the window seems to explain that B&H means "Better health." They were actually the initials of the original owners, Abie Bergson and Jack Heller, who opened the lunch counter around 1937. Bergson was an aspiring actor and the B&H, during the tail end of Yiddish theater on Second Avenue, was patronized by stars such as Molly Picon and Maurice Schwartz. Mr. Heller was succeeded in the partnership by Sol Hausman. Bergson sold the luncheonette in the early 1970s, and by September of 1978, it went bankrupt. In May of that year, Boti Sherman, a partner in a lower-Manhattan construction company, bought the assets, fixtures, and name with a ten-year lease.

It's a small, narrow store that seats twenty-six, with a counter that accommodates thirteen, yet Leo Ratnofsky, a counterman since 1940, estimated at least one thousand customers on a typical day. He was part of a five-man team of countermen serving affordable food — breakfast starting at 5:30 am — and acting as social directors for the ever-changing neighborhood. Customers who left tips over 25 cents received a public shout-out of "Jumbo jockey!" Ratnofsky recalled Maurice Schwartz, of the Yiddish Art Theatre, complaining "that there were more people at the counter of the B&H than in

480

481

BY TIM HARROD

No, Virginia

Inside the stocking there is only…emptiness

In 1897, *The New York Sun* published a letter by eight-year-old Virginia O'Hanlon and its response by Editor Francis Church, an exchange which would grow to be a perennial classic.

As Yuletide sentiment once more pervades the land, and seeing that *The Sun* has long since set from the journalistic landscape, we take great pride in reprinting the plaintive inquiry of a curious child and its wise response.

············ ◆ ············

Dear Editor: I am 8 years old. Some of my little friends say there is no Santa Claus. Papa says, "If you see it in The Sun *it's so." Please tell me the truth: Is there a Santa Claus?*
—Virginia O'Hanlon
115 West Ninety-Fifth Street

Virginia, you are eight years of age and you are asking whether a magical flying man visits multiplied-millions of homes in a single night? I suggest you listen to these "little friends" of yours. They sound pretty sharp, and if you and they are ever lost on a camping trip, I vehemently suggest putting them in charge. But let me approach your inquiry in this way: On Christmas Eve, do you leave some manner of food out for Santa, as many children customarily do? Now, having never met you and knowing nothing about the O'Hanlon family: it is a kind of food your Papa enjoys, isn't it? *Do you see where I am going with this?*

No, Virginia, there is no Santa Claus. Your home will not be surreptitiously invaded by a monumentally wealthy elf-man who rewards your fealty to his capricious moral code with trinkets and baubles; You get enough of that *ad hoc* moralizing, I am sure, from your parents, schoolmasters and clergy with their selfish and competing notions of how childhood "ought to" be.

Neither, Virginia, is there a Jesus Christ, nor a Jehovah, nor any force benevolent or malevolent which judgmentally supervises us from afar. Though you own the pleasure of total privacy in your personal affairs, know that this is neither gift nor privilege, but a happenstance artifact of how the universe has accreted, and the price of this liberty is a coldly indifferent cosmos which would not so much recover from your immediate death as fail to notice it, not for a thousandth of a second, nor one-tenth of one-ten-thousandth of a second.

You will one day grow to adulthood and become a parent yourself, and in that time, to your own little ones, you will perpetuate the endless lie of Santa Claus, the baroque charade of fearfully bartering obedience for material goods, a manipulative moral *non sequitur* that prepares children for a lifetime as dutiful consumers. And I can no more condemn an exercise that makes a meaningless life more bearable than I can condone it. But since my vocation is in the dissemination of facts, and since you in your precocity have thought to pose the question, duty compels me to disabuse you of this puerile myth. In a way, your childhood ends with you reading this response, young Virginia; I apologize to be the agent of your expulsion from the Paradise of ignorance into the bleak, grey corridor of adulthood that leads only to death. But I am shackled to my own conscience—rather than any concern for you, a total stranger—and must see to it that I sleep as easily as manageable to-night. May the Void embrace you with minimal sting.

— *The Editor.* **B**

TIM HARROD *(@quizmonster) has written for* **The Onion, Late Night with Conan O'Brien,** *and* **HQ Trivia.** *So, you know, there's that. We reprint this piece every holiday because Mike loves it.*

The Masked Wrestlers of Mexico
by Seymour Chwast

A set of six, signed, 8.5" x 11" giclée prints on archival paper. Inspired by the revered tradition of Mexican wrestlers wearing creative and menacing masks.

Limited edition prints. Each set of six, $350.

Purchase Online at
www.pushpininc.com/gallery/pushpin-products

Javier

César

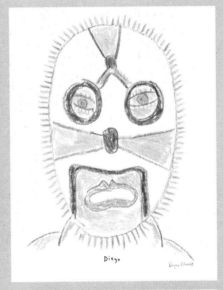
Diego

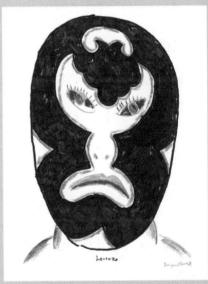
Lorenzo

Ignacio

Juaquin

Potty training can be a PRICKLY issue.

Laugh out loud with this picture book about a family *attempting* to potty train their new pet porcupine, from *New Yorker* cartoonist Tom Toro. You may almost wet your pants giggling.

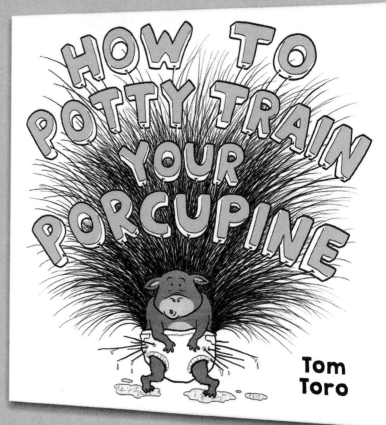

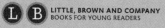 LITTLE, BROWN AND COMPANY BOOKS FOR YOUNG READERS #HowtoPottyTrainYourPorcupine I LBYR.com

WAITING for GODOVID

KUPER

DO YOU KNOW GINGER?

WE DO.

Created as the perfect conclusion to a great meal, Barrow's Intense is a cold pressed ginger liqueur, handcrafted in Brooklyn using more than 200lbs of fresh ginger per batch. Serve it over ice or add it to your favorite cocktail.

44 proof/22% ALC/VOL
Gluten Free, Vegan, Kosher Ⓚ

4 Stars/Highly Recommended & Superb
F. Paul Pacult / Spirit Journal Sept 2014

A+
Good Spirits News

94
THE **TASTING** PANEL

"Best in Class"

HANDMADE IN · BROOKLYN ·

BARROW'S

INTENSE

GINGER
LIQUEUR

Handmade in Brooklyn
750 ML   22% Alc/Vol (44 Proof)

barrowsintense.com   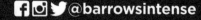 @barrowsintense

It makes no sense in this time of COVID—of institutional and societal trauma; of conspiracies, uncertainty, anger, suffering, and the general uproar over everything—to be presenting several pages of frivolous material just so that you, the reader, will be able to put aside your dread and, for a few moments at least, think about something else. I can see you, you know, and if you are as paranoid as you look right now, my telling you that reading this article will help you press pause on the misery button of your life will definitely seem disingenuous, conspiratorial, fake, even. But fake? Really? Who can say what's real and what's fake anymore?

Santa...By Seurat?

Unless I'm in a Walmart, where they begin playing Christmas music in May, my thoughts don't turn to the holidays until December, when all the leaves have fallen and the polar vortex swirls around the house. Then I'll build a cozy fire, nail the stockings to the fridge, and after a few flagons of grog—'tis the season, y'know—my thoughts will inevitably turn to that most ubiquitous symbol of the holiday spirit, Santa Claus.

It is a little-known fact that Santa Claus has been limned by more fine artists than can squeeze up to a free buffet in Chelsea. The jolly old elf has always been a trusted friend and devoted patron of artists. And in exchange for tubes of paint, sable-hair brushes, or lumps of coal to heat their studios, St. Nick has had his portrait painted by many esteemed artists.

Sure, this sounds like the blather of someone who has had too much grog, and maybe I have, but I don't see *you* writing this introduction, do I? So, yes, this may never really have happened, but if it did happen, if over the centuries Santa Claus was the subject of many artworks by many artists, this is how they would have looked.

No kidding.

—*Rick Meyerowitz*

GEORGES SEURAT, *Santa sur La Grande Jatte.*

MARCEL DUCHAMP,
Santa Descending a Chimney.

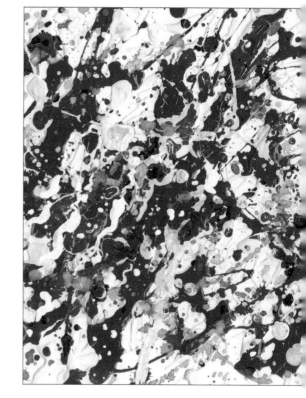

ALBERTO GIACOMETTI,
Walking Santa 1.

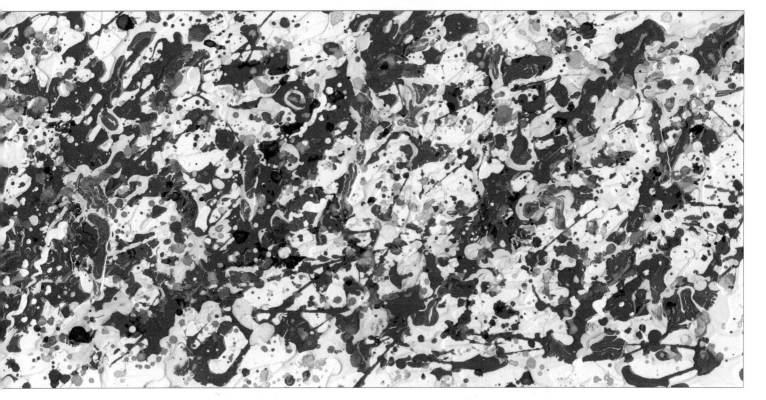

JACKSON POLLOCK, *Red Poles (For Nick).*

VINCENT VAN GOGH, *The Cookie Eater.*

FRANCIS BACON, *Knackered Saint.*

DAMIEN HIRST, *Untitled.*

EDVARD MUNCH, *Insanity Claus.*

ROBERT RAUSCHENBERG, *Mostly Erased de Kooning Drawing of Old Nicky.*

EDWARD HOPPER,
Silent Nighthawks.

**CHRISTO AND
JEANNE-CLAUDE,**
Wrapped Saint.

FRANK GEHRY,
Sketch for North Pole Workshop.

LEONARDO da VINCI, *Il Joculario.*

B

Have Yourself A Monkey Little Christmas

A Holiday Tale of Rex Koko,
Private Clown

It wasn't enough that I was spending five days a week ringing a bell in a ridiculous outfit. It wasn't enough that the snow and slush had soaked my 42s clean through (it takes a week to dry the gunboats out completely, you know). It wasn't enough that I couldn't join the boys down at the Banana Peel for their holiday party, with the roast pig and the flaming shish kabobs and the fire truck and everything.

All that wasn't enough. Now I had to hunt down the creep who stole the Salvation Army kettle right from under my bell-ringing nose, or the name "Rex Koko" would go down in the annals of Christmastime alongside Ebenezer Scrooge and whatever guy it was invented fruitcake.

How'd they cloat the kettle out from under me? I never left my corner, I wasn't drinking, I wasn't asleep (then). There were people everywhere, hustling around doing their shopping.

I thought of the million ways I would murder the lowlife who filched it. But first I'd have to catch him—and how might I do that? The snow around the tripod was pretty much undisturbed, the footprints of the ginks on the street straight and predictable. And you couldn't mistake my duck stompers in the fresh snow. Whoever stole it, did it without leaving any tracks.

First I went up Mardo Street a block and saw nothing, and then went down the block and saw the same. From across the street, though, came a yodel: "Hey Santa! You gonna bring me that pop gun I asked for?"

I was in no mood for wise guys so I didn't answer and walked in the opposite direction. Apparently that wasn't the right response, because I heard the dope start yipping and heading my way. When he was behind me, I turned around, fists ready. And who should I see then but my oldest pal, Bingo, flanked on either side by a couple of tanked-up bally girls.

"Hey Santa, I asked you a question. You gonna break an old clown's heart again? I been askin' you for a pop gun for 30 years."

"Have you been a good little boy?" I asked, in a pretty bad Santa voice.

"I dunno, Whadda you say, girls? Was I good?"

His partners giggled and swooned. "And if I weren't good," Bingo claimed, "stamina still counts for somethin'!"

"Bingo, take it easy. I ain't Santa."

"What? Then put 'em up, ya bum! What've you done with the real Santa?"

I couldn't tell if Bingo was drunk or just being Bingo, so I pulled my beard down and looked him square in the eye. "Bingo, look, it's me, Rex Koko, your favorite joey."

The flash of recognition in his eyes quickly turned to pain. "Aw Rex, are you telling me you're the one been stiffin' me all these years? One lousy pop gun! How could you?"

Bingo started to cry, and the two jills turned, ready to gut me. This was no time to tell Bingo the facts about Kris Kringle. "Okay, Bingo, ya got me. I'll find ya that pop gun. But first, Santa needs your help."

"Sorry, Santa-Rex, I've heard that song before. I'm skint. Go borrow from someone else."

"Not that kind of help. Have you seen ol' Santa on this corner ringin' his bell?"

"Why sure!"

"Well, what would you say if I told you that some crumb bum stole Santa's kettle? It's like a Christmas mystery, Bingo. The can and the cash are gone, but there's no footprints in the snow anywhere around it."

"Oh, that's an easy one, Santa pal. It must've been a coupla angels come swooping down."

Oh, this was going to go well. "Bingo, think about

············ ◆ ············

James Finn Garner *wrote* **Politically Correct Bedtime Stories** *and the clown noir series starring Rex Koko. His eponymous website is named for him.*

it. Why would angels have to steal from the Salvation Army?"

"Maybe to boost their pensions."

"What else could come from up above, like an angel, but's not an angel?"

"A ghost. A cloud. An eagle...or a monkey."

A light flickered on. "Bingo, you might be onto something." In fact, I knew one Top Town local with lots of colleagues of the simian persuasion.

"Well, glad to solve the case for you, Santa. Now get me that pop gun or I'm gonna tell everyone you're really Rex and blow your whole grift."

After Bingo and his chippies tottered off in the direction of the next gin mill, I left my empty tripod standing on the corner and went to pay a visit to Lem Torretson at the Monkey Hostel. I couldn't imagine a nice old dope like Lem being involved with this, but I had to start somewhere.

I shoved my bell in my pocket and headed west. All around me were signs that Top Town was trying to get into the

Christmas spirit. Over at the 10-in-1, The Amazing Electro was swallowing brightly colored strings of lights like they were strings of popcorn, while Gordie the Dog-Faced Boy teamed up with Eli the Fat Man for a little Santa/Rudolph schtick. But judging from people's expressions, it had been a rough end to another rough year. So what else was new in our little termite paradise? That didn't give anyone the right to glom my kettle.

Over on Fratellini Street, I banged on the door of the hostel. The place was sealed up tight; everyone in the joint hated cold weather. Some of the chimps had coats, but the little monks with the long tails had to stay inside, else they'd turn into furry little popsicles. There was no sound from inside, which was strange because this place was always full of screeches and grunts. I banged on the door again:

"Lem! Get out here! I gotta bone to pick with you!"

The wind was the only sound in the

quiet night. Then the latch of the door moved and the door opened. I expected to see Lem's skinny, spooky face peek out of the opening. Instead, about two feet lower, I saw the hairy mug of one of the chimps. He stared at me for an uncomfortably long time, then motioned me in. I think. Anyway, he went back inside, and I followed.

The chimp led me down a short hallway lit by some bare bulbs. Man, the stench was a killer; it takes an awful lot for me to gag, and I almost did. Down the hall the chimp turned into a doorway. Inside, I saw Lem lying in bed, looking paler than usual. He seemed startled to see me.

"Koko. What do you want? You look like a fever dream, in that Santa get-up."

"Merry Christmas, Lem. You're not looking so good yourself."

"It's just the flu. It'll pass," he said with a wheeze.

"Then I got a question for you: Are all your tenants present and accounted for?"

"Sure they are. Why?"

"You're so certain, lying on your sickbed here, that every one of these monks is sitting around and picking lice exactly where they're supposed to?"

"You got something to say, spit it out, clown."

So I told him about my bell-ringing, and the kettle filching, and how the lack of footprints brought me to his door.

Lem dismissed my theory with a weak raspberry. "That's a stretch. None of my babies have been out of the hostel all night. I would've heard it. Isn't that right, Fanny?"

He looked at the chimp squatting at the foot of his bed, and she looked back at him with those round Coca-Cola eyes. Then she looked down, and turned her back. Chimps may be a lot of things, but they're lousy liars.

"Fanny...?"

"Looks like something's going on behind your back, Lem. Now, if you'll just hand over my kettle with the ske-jeema intact, I'll forget this ever happened, though I won't forget the smell."

Sternly, Lem told Fanny to see if the kettle was around the hostel. She shuffled out, while I stayed by Lem's bedside. He coughed enough to wake the dead. "You don't sound so hot, Lem. You sure it's only the flu? You seen a croaker?"

"And how would I pay him if I saw him? This might be the flu or it might not, but....well, what can you do?"

Off in the other rooms was a lot of screaming and pounding. It sounded like Fanny had found the missing article, but the others were protesting about handing it over. In a minute she dragged it into Lem's room and set it at my feet. Her face was sadder than a rained-out birthday, and she gave me a look that said there was a lot more going on around here.

"All right, Lem, what's the kaye fabe? Your monks don't ever get in trouble, hardly, and yet here they are, stealing from the poor. You in hot water? You got enough to pay the rent?"

"That's my business, Koko, and none of yours."

"C'mon, Lem, we've always been square..."

"I tell ya, nothing is going on. You got your kettle, now leave me in peace—I feel a sneeze coming on."

"All right, Lem, I'll scram. If it's any consolation, whatever comes next is your own doing." I meant that to be comforting, but it didn't come out that way.

I picked up my kettle and walked out of the room, headed for the front door. In the hallway, from out of the darkness came a hairy hand, holding a piece of paper. The animal in the darkness was shoving it into my palm insistently. I opened the paper and read it as best I could by the light bulb. It was a letter from someone named Sammy Schratt. With maximum nastiness, Schratt told Lem that their previous arrangement was now null and void, and if Lem didn't have all his back rent paid up, he and all his monks would be kicked out in the street at the end of the month.

And here's where the ho-ho comes in: It was dated December 24. Today. Christmas Eve.

In the shadows around me, I could see the dark shapes of the chimps and monks. They gathered around me in a circle. Some picked at my trouser leg sadly. They were all waiting for me to do something.

It didn't take long for the monkeys and me to work out a plan—but could they stick to it? I'm a professional, but it ain't easy working with these brats,

"Just what other kind of Christmas WOULD *you be dreaming of, Johnson?"*

I tell ya.

It wasn't a dukey run over to Sammy Schratt's place, so we made it there in under 15 minutes. Darkness had fallen good and hard, and his neighborhood wasn't graced with much in the way of street lamps. Even in the dark, you could tell Schratt was a tightwad, with a frame house in a barren yard and a chain link fence around it. I didn't know anything about his business or lack of it, but throwing a bunch of apes out in the cold on Christmas Eve didn't raise him much in my estimation.

We climbed the fence and took our places. I peeked in the window and saw Schratt sitting at his desk, papers everywhere, drinking a tall tumbler of something dark. Perfect. I gave the signal for the spectacle to begin.

One of the monks gave a hard rap on the front door. Schratt looked up from his papers, puzzled, then slowly got up to answer. When he got to the door, no one was there—but in the meantime, we pried open his window and sent in one of the smaller chimps to drop a Mickey Finn into Schratt's drink. Before the skinflint got back to his chair, the chimp had to hide himself and stay

hidden until the rest of us entered. As I watched, the little simian did his job perfectly, and soon Schratt sat back down, none the wiser.

I waited three minutes, then ran around to the back. There I found another window unlatched, so I let myself and the rest of the monks in. We were in the kitchen and spartan though it was, the prospect of food sent the monks into a scurrying frenzy, running here, sniffing there, opening cupboards. Our plan was in danger of falling apart before it began. I hissed at them to stay focused, then did my best silent mime at them to "chew quietly."

Precious seconds ticked away, but it would've been worse if Schratt's pantry were full. I had no choice but to cut them some slack. What must it be like, being a monkey in a new kitchen? Probably like being let out of prison and shipped to a harem.

Fanny gave a final belch and we carried on. The hallway was dark, and a little creepy. We tiptoed down quiet as a fire drill and entered the room. There was Schratt, sitting in his easy chair now, with his hand to his forehead, trying to stop the room from spinning.

One of the monks went up and tugged on his sleeve.

When he opened his eyes, he could barely make his mouth work. Finally he spat out, "Sh..Shanta?"

"Ho ho. Got it in one, Einstein."

"Shanta? What...What's going on? Ooohh, I don't feel well."

"What you're feeling there is the after-effects of your poor behavior this year. When kids are naughty, they don't get any presents. When grown-ups are naughty, I can pitch 'em a touch of food poisoning."

"Can't believe it... the real Shanta?" I leaned back and made with a very hearty "Ho ho ho!" Unfortunately, it sent me into a coughing fit and completely freaked out the monkeys.

This didn't go unnoticed by Sammy Schratt. "Who...Who are all these...?"

"Ya don't recognize my elves? They always travel with me, especially in rough neighborhoods like this one."

"Why...are they wearing... fur coats?"

"Because it's freezing out, that's why. Running around in leotards will get you the flu."

Schratt was sweating all over, red eyes and pale skin. I don't think he looked all that good normally, but the Mickey Finn wasn't helping. "You said... I've been naughty?"

"Why the hell do you think I came over here? You've gotta get on the straight and narrow, Samuel. I hear you've been mean and heartless to some of your friends? Particularly one Lem Torretson."

"Lem?"

"Yeah, Lem. You're going to throw him and his family out on the street on Christmas?"

"Wha...family...Lem doesn't have....?"

Suddenly there was a crash in the kitchen. I ducked my head down the hallway and shouted, "Hey, ya little poop-flinger, get back in here!"

Schratt was getting more confused by the minute. "Poop-flinger...."

"Who said 'poop-flinger'? His name is ... Boot-Jingler...And he's gotta quit raiding people's iceboxes! Now Samuel, Santa is very busy at the time of year. I need to wrap things up and fly away."

"What ... should I do...?"

"You gotta sign this letter saying that Lem can continue to stay in his place for the rent of one dollar per year, ad infinitum. Notice the Latin? That means it's legal."

"But....my business..."

"Your business will be worth nanty if you don't straighten up and fly right. You do not want Santa Claus hounding you, pal, believe me. I've got people everywhere. I can make your life pretty miserable, ho de ho de ho de ho."

I reached into my pocket and pulled out the letter I prepared—then Boot Jingler grabbed it. "Hey!" The little demon ran around the room with it, waving it, chewing it. All his buddies thought this was great fun and gave chase.

"Santa...your elves... smell funny..."

"Hey, you try living at the North Pole for a while—come back here, furball!—the showers are pretty cold."

After losing my hat, breaking a bowl and knocking over Schratt's hat rack twice, I finally got the paper back from the monk in one piece. "Now, Samuel, you've gotta trust me on this. If you do one good deed, it doesn't just sit there. It multiplies, right? That's what yours truly's all about. Now, sign this page and we'll get out of your hair. It's eight o'clock—we should be flying over Montana by now, right, little elves?"

"I don't know...."

"Listen, sign it," I snarled, "or I leave little Boot-Jingler here to keep you company until you do."

On cue, Boot-Jingler screeched so loud we both jumped out of our skins.

Latin or no, I was under no illusions about the legality of what I'd gotten Schratt to sign. On the other hand, it was as binding as the poison-pen letter he'd sent to Lem. And people with guilty consciences tend to believe in superstition. All in all, I figured this arrangement would sit okay with him; if Schratt wanted to contest it in any way, he'd have to claim that he signed it under duress from Santa and his monkey elves, which would make him look like a real Rockefeller.

Lem was still asleep when the monks and I got back. He looked a little better unconscious, so maybe he was out of the woods. We put the letter under Lem's pillow, a nice little surprise for him on Christmas morning.

"All right, you four-handed bums, I've done what I could for you guys. Now I want my skejeema back."

To a monk, they acted like they didn't know what I was talking about.

"The kettle. My bucket with the dough in it."

Still nothing.

"Listen, you little fakers, give me back my kettle or......"

Finally, little Fanny dragged the kettle out from beneath Lem's bed. It scraped heavily, which pleased me.

"About time," I said, "and it better not be light."

When I stuck my hand in, I felt a little something more than money. Something warm and soft, and definitely not gingerbread. The monkeys began laughing their heads off.

Merry Christmas, ya hairy devils. **B**

"It was never about the presents—it's about the power."

Elvis is Alive and Well
inside these pages

Seymour Chwast

Steven Brower

Seymour Chwast
Steven Brower

The Mighty
ELVIS
A Graphic Biography

Contents

www.yoebooks.com

WHERE WERE YOU IN '92?

SLOUCHERS

A NOVEL BY E.L. LESSERT

BASED ON THE SCREENPLAY BY MAC McHENRY

USED

OUT NOW

BY MIKE SACKS

Hell, American Style

Someday, we'll all look back at 2020, and laugh.
Until then, there's **Ron Hauge.**

For more, follow Ron on Instagram: @ron_hauge.
His new cartoon book will be released this fall.

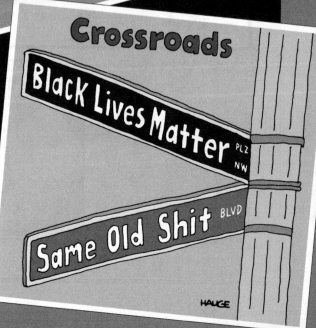

A limited edition of 25 Giclée prints on archival stock, 8" x 10", signed by R. O. Blechman and Nicholas Blechman, is available for $325, postage included. Inquire at ro@roblechman.com.

They'll go fast!

THE "EYES" HAVE IT!

THANKSGIVING HAS ALWAYS SEEMED A SOMEWHAT STRANGE HOLIDAY TO ME, DUE TO ITS INNATE BORINGNESS. AS A BOY I WOULD WAKE UP EARLY IN THE MORNING BEFORE EVERYONE ELSE AND SET MYSELF UP IN FRONT OF THE BLACK AND WHITE TELEVISION TO WATCH THE THANKSGIVING PARADE TAKING PLACE IN NEW YORK CITY. BEING IN LOS ANGELES WITH THE THREE HOUR TIME DIFFERENCE IT WAS PREDAWN. THERE I SAT CROSS-LEGGED ON THE FLOOR, THE ODD GLOW OF THE TEE-VEE ILLUMINATING THE ROOM, DRINKING ORANGE JUICE AS THE PAGEANT UNFOLDED. I WAS FASCINATED BY THE FLOATS BECAUSE THEY WERE MADE OF FLOWERS. THEY SEEMED SO PRETTY AND FRAGILE IN THEIR JUXTAPOSITION TO THE GROTESQUE GIANT BALLOONS WAFTING ABOVE THEM. SOME OF THE GIANT BALLOONS WERE RECOGNIZABLE CARTOONS, A LOT OF THEM WEREN'T, AND WERE VERY CREATIVE, WEIRD, AND EVEN SCARY. THESE WERE MY FAVORITES. EVEN THIS BECAME BORING AND I BEGAN TO WONDER WHY PEOPLE DIDN'T LET GO OF THEM SO THEY COULD JOIN THE STRATOSPHERE. WHY DIDN'T SOMEONE POP THEM, SENDING THEM BUZZING AND CAREENING ABOVE THE CROWD LIKE A FLOCK OF FLATULENT PELICANS? THESE THINGS NEVER HAPPENED. THE THANKSGIVING DAY PARADE WAS STUCK IN MELANCHOLY STODGINESS. PERHAPS IT SEEMED GLAMOROUS ON COLOR TEE-VEE. MANY YEARS LATER I WOULD BE PROVEN QUITE WRONG ABOUT THANKSGIVING WHEN THE DAY BECAME A.......

DESPERADO SHINDIG!

IT HAPPENED IN SEATTLE IN THE LATE 1990'S. THE GRUNGE ERA WAS KAPUT. HEROIN HAS ITS WAY OF DOING THAT, AND THE ARTISTIC PRETENTIONS OF GLOBAL POP CULTURE DOMINANCE LAY IN RUINS, QUICKLY GIVING WAY TO SOMETHING WORSE. MUCH WORSE. THE NEW PRETENTIONS OF THE WORLD WIDE WEB. INSTEAD OF CREATING A CATERWAULING BOMBASTIC DIN TO MAKE ONES FORTUNE, IT WAS NOW BECOMING HIP TO SIT IN A CUBICLE AND TYPE. FOR A START-UP DOT.COM THAT IS. ANGSTY GUITAR SMASHING PAID, BUT NOT AS WELL AS FEISTY MOUSE CLICKING WITH STOCK OPTIONS. SEATTLE'S SMART SET WERE SCRAMBLING FOR THESE GIGS. THE MONEY WAS POURING INTO TOWN THE SAME AS IT DID YEARS EARLIER WHEN RECORD COMPANY EXECUTIVES SWARMED IN FROM POINTS EAST AND SOUTH. ONLY THIS TIME IT WASN'T SHOW BUSINESS MONEY. IT WAS THE INTERNATIONAL LOOT OF INVESTMENT BANKERS AND MEGALOMANIAC NERDS. WHILE ALL OF THIS WAS TRANSPIRING A DIFFERENT SORT OF OLD SCHOOL THIEF HAD COME TO TOWN.

LOSERS.

I'M TELLING YOU, BY 2005 THERE WON'T BE ANY PRINT PUBLICATIONS!! THAT'S THE TRUTH!

SOONER THAN THAT BRO, SOONER THAN THAT!!!

THE HOLLYWOOD BANDIT! THE MEDIA GAVE HIM THIS TITLE BECAUSE HE AND HIS GANG WORE ELABORATE MOVIE MAKEUP FOR DISGUISES. OVER SEVERAL YEARS HE SUCCESSFULLY ROBBED 17 SEATTLE BANKS, STEALING MILLIONS OF DOLLARS. ON A RAINY DARK THANKSGIVING EVE, THE 18TH ROBBERY WENT WRONG. AFTER STEALING OVER ONE MILLION DOLLARS FROM A SEAFIRST BANK BRANCH, THEIR GETAWAY VAN GOT STUCK IN HOLIDAY TRAFFIC. THIS MISHAP ALLOWED THE POLICE TO CATCH UP TO THE GANG SURROUNDING THEIR VAN IN THE RAVENNA NEIGHBORHOOD. A HUGE SHOOTOUT COMMENCED, WOUNDING BOTH OF THE HOLLYWOOD BANDITS COLLEAGUES WHO WERE ARRESTED. THE HOLLYWOOD BANDIT ESCAPED UNSEEN BY THE POLICE. THE FOLLOWING DAY HE WAS STILL ON THE LOOSE WHEN MY WIFE AND I ARRIVED AT A FRIENDS HOUSE IN RAVENNA FOR THANKSGIVING DINNER.

After the ThanksGiving Eve shoot-out, the Hollywood Bandit holed up in a Camper Set on SawHorses in the BackyarD of a House a Few Doors Down the Street from our FrienDs House. The FBI and the SeaHle Police HAD SearcheD For him all night. They HAD even SearcheD that very House and BackyarD but HAD Declined to Search the Camper! ThanksGiving Day the guys who owned the Camper took a sneaky peek.

On ThanksGiving Afternoon just as we were sitting Down to Dinner, a HuGe COMMOTION COMMENCED outsiDe in the Street. ArmoreD vehicles, Police Cars, SWAT teams, and FBI Agents were SwarminG Everywhere right outside the picture winDow. It was Chaos PersonifieD. A Beautiful thing to BeHolD. More Beautiful than a Drum Majorette Procession. This was GoinG to Be a Great Day after all.

HAve Some PArfait Pie! It's my Mom's recipe from COLORADO.

I HAven't HAD PArfait Pie since I was a Little Boy. THAnks!

A Man was YellinG OrDers through a megaphone while Dozens of Officers were GettinG into Position with rifles and pistols Drawn. They HAD a thingamajig that fires tear gas Cannisters to flush him out. The Guy with the Bullhorn rang the Front DoorBell. He said they were EvacuatinG the NeighBors, But not us. They HAD to use our FrienDs House as the "COMMAND" House, Because it sat DiaGonally on the Corner making it iDeal. He said we CoulD stay and enjoy our Dinner. Soon there were a Bunch of Guys on the Stakeout mingling at our Party. Our hostess offereD them Dinner as there was plenty. She was in the true Spirit of the holiDay, as was my wife who offereD Dessert. In Between their HusheD Discussions and the FBI honcho stepping out to Bellor threats at the Bandit, they joineD in our HoliDay festivities.

BroaDcastinG Live from the Hollywood Bandit ShowDown!

You poor thinG! On your next Break Come insiDe for some Dinner and Dessert.

MayHem with your Meal the most ExcitinG THANKSGIVING ever!

SUCH A BEASTLY FEAST inDeeD!

Four Hours HAD passeD and it was Dark. A Television news Crew was outsiDe on the Front Lawn interviewinG the FBI and the Police. It was a stalemate. NothinG was HappeninG. The reporter was Frustrated and DurinG Breaks he was firing up a HuGe CiGar, puffinG and pacinG in the rain. They fired tear gas into the Camper, But the Bandit did NOT Come out. SuDDenly the SounD of GunfireErupteD!

Like a Hollywood Western, it was. THEY SHOT up the Camper, finally FirinG a tear Gas Cannister into it. When they finally ApproacheD and entereD, the Hollywood Bandit was DeaD from a Self inflicted Gunshot to the HeaD. That pretty much EnDeD the party. The Bandit HAD to know SeaHle traffic is Atrocious and CurseD. So why DiD He ScheDule a BiG Heist for ThanksGiving HoliDay Eve?

B

NOTES FROM A SMALL PLANET

Love stinx • By Rick Geary

PERHAPS I WAS UNWISE TO START DATING AGAIN ...

SO SOON AFTER MY WIFE HAD MOVED OUT.

ONE PARTICULAR LADY ATTRACTED ME IN A MYSTERIOUS WAY.

AND IT SEEMED SHE HAD THE SAME EFFECT ON SEVERAL OTHER GENTLEMEN.

SHE TOOK PLEASURE IN SETTING US TO IMPOSSIBLE TASKS AND QUESTS.

ONE POOR GUY HAD TO RETRIEVE A HAIR FROM THE HEAD OF A CERTAIN MOVIE STAR.

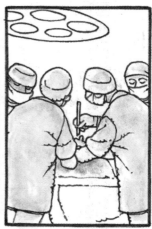

FOR MY PART, I UNDERWENT A PROCEEDURE TO HAVE MY HEART REMOVED.

I INTENDED, FOR HER BIRTHDAY, TO PRESENT IT TO HER ON A SATIN PILLOW.

BUT BEFORE I COULD, ONE OF HER OTHER SUITORS SWOOPED DOWN ON GOLDEN WINGS ...

AND CARRIED HER OFF TO AN EXOTIC DESTINATION!

NOW WHAT'LL I DO WITH THIS HEART?

B

THE KRONINGER COLLECTION

Treasures from one man's fabulous stash of pop culture ephemera. • *By Stephen Kroninger*

KEY: **1** Marx Brothers *TIME* cover (1932) **2** Set of *Wild Style* film promotional buttons (1983) **3** Matt Groening promotional button (1985) **4** Mets beer coaster (1969) **5** Jackie Robinson Button (1947) **6** Batman charm bracelet (1966) **7** Bill Griffith "Zippy" button **8** WMFU "Nancy" button, art by Mark Newgarden (c. 1980s) **9** Double-faced Martin & Lewis puppet. (c.1950s) **10** *New York Post* newspaper kiosk poster. During the newspaper strike in 1978, the *Post* distributed these pink posters displaying what would have been their headline for that day. The rock star in ques-

tion is Sid Vicious of the Sex Pistols. 12 3/4 x 17 3/4. **11** Newport Jazz Festival commemorative plate featuring two of my favorite artists, Louis Armstrong and Duke Ellington. (1957) 9.23" diameter. Come to think of it, I'm quite fond of Benny Goodman's trios and quartets from 1936-38, too! **12** Kim Deitch "Sunshine Girl" button promoting his comic in *The East Village Other* (1967) **13** *RAW Magazine* promo button, art by Gary Panter (1989) **14** Popeye soap on a rope, country of origin and date unknown. *NOTE: Items are not to scale.*

B

visit
www.**rosenworld**.com
for
Sneakers, Signed Books,
Melty Jewels
and Original Artwork
by **Laurie Rosenwald**, First Pancake,
Occasional Swede
& America's
Favorite Bystander

and to name
but just a few:
RED
Yellow
gReen
written and illustrated **blue** by laurie rosenwald

laurie rosenwald
all the wrong people have self-esteem
an inappropriate book for young ladies *
* or frankly, anybody else

a blank book with useful stuff in it
NEW YORK noTe Book
GUIDEBOOK + JOURNAL + SKETCHBOOK
by LAURIE ROSENWALD

"Laurie's voice is fresh sounding,
funny, and completely her own." -David Sedaris

P.S. MUELLER THINKS LIKE THIS

The cartoonist/broadcaster/writer is always walking around, looking at stuff • By P.S. Mueller

THE BIG DRUMMER BOY

FROSTY'S SUMMER HOME

THIS YEAR YOU SHOULD ASK SANTA FOR SOMETHING OTHER THAN A LOOK AT HIS TITS.

P.S. MUELLER is Staff Liar of *The American Bystander*.

ROZ'S MARVELOUS COLLAGES

Japanese matchbox covers from anonymous artists, 1920-1940 • By Roz Chast

B

Love, and Other Weird Things

A book of cartoons by one of your favorite artists,
Rich Sparks

You don't want to miss this book because important people are
talking about it.

"I'm actually trying to get out of the 'blurb game.' Unless it's for
my kids, or someone I owe a shit ton of money to."
—Roz Chast, NY Times best selling cartoonist

"Try not to laugh. I double-dog dare ya!"
—David Yow, a very famous musician and actor

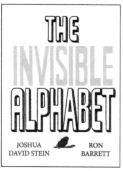

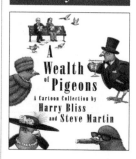

Rasika Boice

WRITER & ILLUSTRATOR
Through my work, I love to share the silly, scary, strange, and sweet parts of life, exploring the grey areas in (mostly) black and white. To purchase a drawing, collaborate, or simply say "Hi!", please do get in touch at **rasika.boice@gmail.com**.

Adrian Bonenberger

AFGHAN POST: A Memoir
"This is a book that will bring the madness and beauty of combat right down into your shaking hands."—**Anthony Swofford**
Available at **Amazon**.

www.wrath-bearingtree.com

TWITTER: @AdrianBonenber1

Chris Bonno

"Coffee Break for Ol' Blue Eyes"

FINE ARTIST/COMEDIAN
For original art inquiries, follow & DM me on Instagram: **@chrisbonnoart**
For prints, go to **bonnoart.storenvy.com**

George Booth

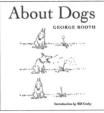

Available at **Amazon**.

Zack Bornstein

"*Women's Day New Zealand* once reported that Bornstein was dating Emma Stone, which was flattering, but later issued a correction, which was devastating."
MG sez: Absolutely go follow **@ZackBornstein** on Twitter.

Lexy Borowitz

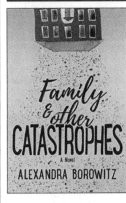

FAMILY AND OTHER CATASTROPHES
"A zany, heartfelt, and laugh-out-loud funny debut."
—*HelloGiggles*
Available at **Amazon**.

Jennifer Boylan

Jennifer Boylan's column appears in *The New York Times* on alternate Wednesdays.

www.jenniferboylan.net

TWITTER: @jennyboylan

GOOD BOY: My Life in Seven Dogs
"Beautiful, tender, and utterly engaging, *Good Boy* measures out Boylan's life in dog years. The result is a gorgeous memoir, full of heart and insight."—*Susan Orlean*
Available at **Powell's**.

Okay, so at this point, I realized that I was **totally not** going to have time to hand-design a Classified ad for all our 300 *Bystander* contributors before this issue needed to go to press. So I'm going to stop being alphabetical, and fill out the page with ones that people have already sent copy for. I will do the others for #19, promise!
Your Enthusiastic but Overworked Editor & Publisher

Diane Baldwin

FREE PHOTOJOURNALISM E-BOOK
Download at
www.store.blurb.comebooks/455989-come-as-you-are

Andrew Barlow

FREE PHOTOJOURNALISM E-BOOK
Download at
www.store.blurb.comebooks/455989-come-as-you-are

Dylan Brody

You *need* this book for the holidays.
RELATIVELY PAINLESS
"If your family is anything like mine, I am so, so sorry."
www.dylanbrody.com/painless

Burns & Folta

A NEWSLETTER OF HUMOROUS WRITING
www.tinyletter.com/humorouswriting
A weekly newsletter by Luke Burns and James Folta

Ryan Nyburg

SYNODUS HORRENDA
is a podcast about death, dying and the dead. Exploring stories from history, art and popular culture to show the myriad of ways death influences society.
Now available on Apple Podcasts.

Bob Eckstein

NEW BOOKS ON SALE NOW!
All's Fair in Love & War: The Ultimate Cartoon Book and *The Elements of Stress and the Pursuit of Happy-ish in this Current Sh*tstorm.*
Both available at **BobEckstein.com**
Sign up there for my FREE newsletter. You can follow me on Twitter/FB/Instagram: @BobEckstein

Zoe Matthiessen

THE LAST STRAW
"This book is a triumph—a luminous, witty story that is easy to grasp and discuss with our kids and everyone else. A brave, brainy, strong moral statement and stunningly beautiful! An instant classic."—*Steve Brodner*
Available January 5 from
NORTH ATLANTIC BOOKS

PREORRER NOW from
Amazon or **Powell's**.

Chris Dingman

HOW TO BELIEVE IN SCIENCE AND ALSO IN SOMETHING BEYOND
Five Essays on How Science Can Coexist with Spirituality.
www.SparkWrites.com

Patrick Kennedy

A GIFT TO INSPIRE YOUR FAVORITE RUNNERS!

BRICKLAYER BILL: The Untold Story of the Workingman's Boston Marathon, by Patrick L. Kennedy and Lawrence W. Kennedy, brings to life one of the toughest, most colorful trailblazers of the road game. "Bricklayer Bill" Kennedy survived a five-story fall, a rail-riding mishap, typhoid fever, and more as he sought glory in the nation's premier marathon a century ago. Foreword by Bill Rodgers.
Available at www.umass.edu/umpress
As heard on NPR's "Only a Game."

Risa Mickenberg

JESUS H CHRIST AND THE FOUR HORNSMEN OF THE APOCALYPSE
invite you to sign up to preview their new musical sh*tstorm *Glass Bikini* presented by Seymour Hare. "An odd blend of Sixpence None The Richer, Arcade Fire and New Pornographers if they were all fronted by Amy Sedaris."—*Pop Matters*
Sign up at
www.jesushchristrocks.com

TAXI DRIVER WISDOM
20th Anniversary Edition from Chronicle Books
http://tiny.cc/taxidriverwisdom

EGG: An anti-family comedy. 100% Fresh on Rotten Tomatoes
On Hulu, Amazon & iTunes
http://tiny.cc/eggthefilm

Lydia Oxenham

LYD-LIFE CRISIS: A Bi-Weekly Crisis in 200 Words or Less
www.tinyletter.com/lydiaoxenham
I can't poop on vacation. This is a crisis. To read about this crisis and more, subscribe to my newsletter!

That's it for this issue. Tune in next time for MORE MORE MORE Classified Ads! (Like, seriously. There will be a LOT.)

WHEN I STARTED OUT IN THIS BUSINESS, THERE MUST'VE BEEN OVER A HUNDRED GODS UP HERE. NO KIDDING

MOST ARE GONE NOW, EVEN THE BIGGIES LIKE THOR AND ZEUS. BUT BY ME —KNOCK WOOD— BUSINESS COULDN'T BE BETTER.

IT'S 'CAUSE I HAVE SUCH A WONDERFUL CLIENTELE...Y'CAN'T BEAT JEWS AND CHRISTIANS WHEN IT COMES TO LOYALTY.

F'RINSTANCE, SAY A PLANE GOES DOWN IN A STORM. THEY NEVER BLAME ME FOR THE DISASTER. NEVER. ON THE OTHER HAND...

...IF ANYONE LIVES THROUGH IT, THE FIRST THING HE'LL SAY IS "IT'S A MIRACLE! ONLY THE HAND OF GOD SAVED ME."

IT'S REALLY TOUCHING...THEY'VE READ ABOUT THE MIRACLES I DID IN THE OLD DAYS, AND THEY ASSUME I STILL DO THAT SORT OF THING.

BUT YOU KNOW WHAT WOULD HAPPEN IF I STARTED TO DO REAL MIRACLES AGAIN? I'LL TELL YOU...

...I'D BE UP NIGHT AND DAY, DAY AND NIGHT, ANSWERING PRAYERS FOR WHO KNOWS WHAT. LET'S FACE IT...

...I CAN'T KEEP THOSE KIND OF HOURS ANYMORE.

ED SOREL (edwardsorel@gmail.com) is the author and illustrator of **Mary Astor's Purple Diary** (2016). A collection of his drawings, **Profusely Illustrated**, is scheduled for 2021.